Welcome to the magical world of animals! Here, every stroke and color is an adventure full of fun and learning. This book was made with all the care and dedication for you. May your colors fill these images with life and joy, creating special memories that will be cherished forever. Have fun coloring and exploring this enchanting universe!

Binho Ferrer

2024

This Book Belongs to:

Test Color Page

9 798884 954830